LIFE INTERRUPTED:

Dr. Dua's Survival Guide

By Dr. Manu Dua

Foreword and Epilogue by Dr. Parul Dua Makkar

LAUREL ELITE BOOKS
Laurel Elite Books
Claremont, NH

Front cover photo credit Arti Panchal Photography

Life Interrupted: Dr. Dua's Survival Guide
Written by Dr. Manu Dua
Copyright © 2021 by Dr. Parul Dua Makkar

Laurel Elite Books
1 Foster Place
Claremont, NH 03743
www.LaurelElitecom

Additional copies of this book may be purchased at:
www.LaurelElite.com

Front cover photo credit: Arti Panchal Photography
Book design: YellowStudios

Paperback ISBN: 978-1-7360587-1-8
Library of Congress Control Number: 2021914596

Printed in the United States of America

To Ma and Papa,
eternally grateful.

CONTENTS

FOREWORD

This book is a series of blogs which were written by my younger brother, Dr. Manu Dua. He wrote these as he battled metastatic cancer and was in the last stages of his disease. He was 34 at the time. This book is a testament of how he was more than the illness that took him. Manu put up a phenomenal fight. Cancer doesn't only affect the person who has it, but also the village that surrounds him/her. The suffering doesn't end when the person passes; the family suffers still with the loss long after. Sometimes it's hard to travel this arduous journey alone. Others who haven't been through it don't necessarily understand the anguish, even though they are supportive. I certainly didn't until I lost Manu. It was hard to accept and find happiness again. Time heals, and I try to give myself that time: time to let go of him, but not his memories.

This book is also a dedication to the unwavering love, kindness, devotion, and support of our parents. They are the pillars of our lives, without whom Manu and I could not be who we are today.

Manu was my younger and only sibling. His death still feels unreal, even though our family watched him suffer and fade away within two years of diagnosis. Manu started writing in September of 2020. In December that year, he and I talked about getting published. I asked him if he wanted to write a book on how he enjoyed driving because he was in control of the car, unlike his destiny which he couldn't control, and tie it to his blogs. He said no, he had no anger or loss of control due to cancer, but he had come to terms. He wanted this to be a series of blogs to share his experience and give some comfort to others.

Manu had a gift of writing eloquently. He was very verbal and open about his journey. This book was in the works during his last days. I would have liked him to see his dream a reality, but time was not on our side. Even though he isn't here today, I wanted to make this book to come to light in his honor.

These blogs carry a lot of insight, and may provide you some comfort if you or a loved one has experienced loss. They give insight to how we chase dreams for other people, trophies, or materialistic things, yet it may not bring us inner peace. How to be calm when the world falls around you, to acknowledge what and who truly matters in life, to find that precious reason and hold onto it. Life doesn't come with guarantees, and things don't go as planned, yet we muster the strength to carry on. Let go of fear and hold on to hope. After reading these pearls of Manu's wisdom and resilience, I hope that you get a chance to reflect and maybe do some soul searching.

This is Manu's legacy.

Dr. Parul Dua Makkar
June 2021

FROM THE AUTHOR

Hi, my name is Dr. Manu Dua. I would like to take the time to speak to you about my life story, which is not only remarkable, but almost borderline ridiculous insofar that it is hard to believe it is real. I do not believe any human being deserved to suffer so much in such a short time, but at the same time I am deeply grateful that I am still alive to type these words, and I have a deeply found appreciation for the meaning of life and what is truly important.

In the span of less than a year I have overcome multiple cancer surgeries, chemotherapy, cancer radiation treatment, learned how to speak again, how to eat, how to swallow and chew again, how to walk again due to a torn ACL. I lost some of my hearing, lost my taste for almost 4 months, lost my grandmother, lost a good friend, had my identity stolen, lost my business, and somewhere between all the pain and suffering, all the loss and despair, I found peace and happiness that I had never attained while I was healthy.

The irony in all of this is that as a dentist, I had the fortune and misfortune of finding my own oral cancer on two separate occasions, and without quick intervention and excellent care from a team of Surgeons and Oncologists, I would not be here to write these very words. I had no risk factors, never smoked, and hardly drank; I was just a victim of bad luck.

I had all my treatment for my recurrent cancer during the worldwide COVID-19 pandemic, and had to juggle the responsibilities of managing a dental practice and subsequent sale of said practice during the pandemic, all while undergoing cancer treatment and grieving for my grandmother who passed away just two days after my second diagnosis.

Just as things started to settle in my life and I was recovering from my second round of cancer surgeries and chemo-radiation in the summer, in mid-November as the pandemic raged on, I found out that a follow up scan showed that the cancer had spread to my lungs and outside to my bones. This was absolutely devastating, and meant that I had to find my resolve and fight the cells trying to destroy my own body for the third time. For most people, this would be an occasion to give up, but instead for me it was an occasion to put on the boxing gloves for a third round with this evil disease. The reason being is that I cannot predict the future and whether I will live or die, but what I can control is that I will never give up until my last breath.

It is my sincere hope that I may impart some of the wisdom I have gained from almost dying on multiple occasions to anyone who is going through their own personal struggles in life. I would like to share my story that even in the worst of times, and under the worst of circumstances, the human mind, body, and soul have a remarkable capacity to heal. We are more powerful than we can ever imagine.

Please read more as I go into detail on what can be described as nothing short of a surreal series of events.

LIFE INTERRUPTED

ON HOPE

Hope is one of the most beautiful things in life. We often don't appreciate its beauty until we are placed in ugly, difficult situations where all we are left with is hope. Hope is one of the few emotions that can make us or break us. To lose hope in life is to lose the meaning of life, for it is the spiritual fuel that guides us in this difficult world.

We all have differing concepts of hope and how it plays in our life: hope is an eternal carrot that is dangled before us, and it is healthy for it to be such a way. You see humans have always believed in something greater than ourselves. Some may argue that the pursuit of happiness is to seek meaning beyond our own selves. Hope provides us with an easy- to- grasp concept of something beyond, and the pursuit of such a concept provides us with the energy to pursue our life's goals.

What I learned during some of the most difficult moments of my cancer treatment is that hope is the saviour that gets us through our adversity. The difference is, I realized it mattered not whether what I hoped for would actually be fulfilled, but rather the hope that whatever pain and suffering I was forced to endure would be removed. It mattered not that perhaps the pain and suffering would be replaced by even more pain and suffering;

what mattered was at that point in time I needed an out-of-body experience to get me through those agonizing seconds, minutes, hours, and days.

After suffering more physical and emotional pain than most human beings should ever have to endure, it occurred to me that the only thing that saved me was hope. I feel like what made the difference for me was I used hope as a tool, rather than "blind saving grace" as most people use it for. I used hope daily as a crutch so I could limp out of whatever adversity came my way. Hope is a tool we use to emotionally and mentally live to fight another day. I realized so long as my mind could endure, the body would follow, and the only thing that got me through those dark days was the hope that tomorrow would be a better day.

The secret is that we cannot go back and analyze whether what we hoped for played out in the manner that we expected to, but rather we have to be irrationally optimistic that in this current moment what we hope for will occur in the near future and ignore realities of whether that would be feasible or not.

ON THE ABILITY TO ENDURE

The ability to endure is an elusive concept, and often we are left in awe of those who have endured and continue to endure under the most difficult circumstances. Why is it, then, that some people can endure the most trying of circumstances and come out of them even stronger than before, while others simply wilt under pressure?

That ability to endure can be broken down into what we perceive as the reason for our suffering, and our sense of hope in a tangible better future. Even when we are faced with the most trying of circumstances, what we are willing to endure and overcome is directly correlated with what we perceive to be the ultimate outcome of that suffering. That ultimate outcome is related to our sense of hope. As I have mentioned before, that level of hope does not in any way have to be realistic, but it has to be tangible enough in our minds that we may utilize it as a tool to endure the current circumstances.

It is this utilization of an optimistic future regardless of reality that divides those that are able to persevere under the most difficult of circumstances, and those that succumb under pressure like a wilted daisy. When you are under duress and life seems bleak, you have to seek deep within yourself an internal resolve to live and an internal resolve to persevere, and the truth of the matter is that this resolve does not have to have any rational rhyme or reason. Life is neither rational nor logical, and the only manner in which we can survive the multitudes of adversity that are bestowed upon us is to implement an equally illogical and irrational resolve to persevere.

If we ponder for a moment those that have survived almost implausible scenarios where life's adversity has them upon the ropes, it is an almost illogical and irrational resolve to persevere that actually guides them past these adversities. During all my cancer treatment, I dug deep and created an internal resolve that no matter the odds against me, I would persevere. It did not matter at this point if this came true or not, I simply had to believe it so.

It is important to note that simply because we believe that we will overcome our adversities does not always impact the outcome, and there is a very real reality that we are not able to overcome, and we succumb to what it is that we are fighting against. In that regard, we have to understand that it matters not the outcome of our fight, but rather it matters that if we do overcome our adversity, we will be strong enough to embrace our victory. Sometimes when we do overcome our adversities and we display resolve, if we are not mentally strong to embrace our victory, we may very well be held captive to the emotional and mental trauma of the adversities that challenged our resolve in the first place.

I will never forget the day I spoke with my ENT surgeon about my cancer coming back and the new surgeries, chemo, and radiation I would have to endure to survive. He mentioned that I had a profound outlook on life, because in his practice he had patients that would survive cancer and go on to live long healthy lives physically, but not emotionally. Emotionally, he mentioned since they were enveloped in so much fear about a recurrence, their entire lives revolved around their one traumatic event. In a sense, even when they had endured their adversity they were held captive for an eternity, because they were not mentally prepared to be victorious and overcome their adversity.

The strong ability to endure depends on an infallible belief that we are far greater than the circumstances that ail us, and they are simply a minor setback in what is our ultimate purpose. To live in fear is to fail before we have started, and as my surgeon so profoundly stated, those that survived to live in constant fear may have been better off dying, since a life lived in fear is no life to live at all.

INTERRUPTED THOUGHTS:
ON SUFFERING

I used to believe, and most of us still do, that there is a limit to suffering and pain, and being a good person buys us magical karma points; that the world will unfold magically to protect these good people, and they will sail off into the sunset unscathed. Oh, what a silly thought to have, fighting cancer for the third time, unable to breathe out of one lung, in constant pain with multitudes of painful procedures and tests. I can assure you there is no limit to suffering.

One of the most useful ways to come to terms with the harsh reality of life is that the real world is cruel beyond imagination, and whatever silly fables society may have instilled within us to create some false illusion of safety is completely fabricated.

ON FEAR

Fear is one of those captivating emotions that is both essential for life in the appropriate circumstances, yet when harnessed inappropriately can be both paralyzing in our development, and quite frankly dangerous from both a physical and mental perspective.

From a societal standpoint, we have evolved significantly as a civilization; most of our fears are less driven by a fight- or- flight ability to survive and more of an emotional evolution, where we create environments that both induce our fear and allow it to irrationally perpetuate without any real consequences other than the ones we have convinced ourselves may theoretically happen.

The interesting perspective from which I would like to approach this subject is what happens when we are actually faced with a dangerous and fearful situation, where quite literally the adverse outcome is death. What happens when we realize we spent so much of our time worrying about little adverse outcomes that are inconsequential in the grand scheme of things, and how different our lives would be if we had just captured some of that energy to move past those fears and progress forward in our endeavours?

What would happen to us if we were able to go above and beyond many of our imaginary illusions of fear and transcend those imaginary barriers into a state where even though we understand the risks, we move beyond them because we realize the negative consequences are manageable? It's funny, often we like to throw out the phrase "What's the worst that could happen," and funnily enough, it's when the worst does happen that one really understands what it means to be free. It's very similar to getting a new car; the first time anything happens to your car it hurts deeply, but eventually we get over it and move on, and since that initial fear is overcome, we have the choice to either fix it or let it be. Similarly, I find that in life we have expectations about a sense of normal, be it our hopes, dreams, careers, family life, or relationships, and when these concepts are deeply disturbed in any manner, we are placed in a conundrum. The difference between how we respond to these disturbances in the force, if you will, is how clearly and cleanly we can apply some form of relativity to the situation. Those of us who have the fortune of wisdom unfortunately gained that wisdom through unfortunate events, and in hindsight those painful experiences provide us with a deep sense of stability and appreciation for what's important. Unfortunately, those of us that are more inexperienced in the matters of life, or those that refuse to evolve and mature despite the wealth of their life experiences, react in a manner where small disturbances in life are grossly exaggerated. The argument is not that one should not be fearful, or that simply surviving life's many challenges makes us fearful. The important point is to note the relativity of the concept of fear and react in an appropriate gradient to what disturbs us.

The point is not to be fearless, but rather acknowledge the scale of the fear and apply our personal concept of relativity and react appropriately. Now, we cannot all survive life threatening experiences in order to gain this sense of relativity, but we can vicariously learn through others and gain a sense of appreciation for what really matters. I used to, for example, take my health for granted, and hence I could pursue mundane fears such as not having enough wealth, loneliness, not being socially popular, and so on. It wasn't until I was quite literally fighting for my life that I truly started to appreciate it. It occurred to me that it was not necessary to endure such pain and trauma to learn the simple concept that life is precious. However, I spent so much time embroiled in trivial and non-essential fears that I missed the concept that living well is simply finding tools and strategies to marginalize trivial fears, and finding ways to overcome small and large fears by placing them within a larger framework of relativity. Quite simply put, if it won't kill you, what's the worst that could happen? Live your life my friend, you never know how long you have and what's coming around the corner. Life waits for no one, but your fears will be your only friends if you let them stick around.

ON FAILURE

Life is such an unpredictable and often unfair journey, it is a miracle as to how we are able to survive such extreme swings of good fortune and misfortune that can happen at a moment's notice with no rhyme or reason. Often, we are left in this trap to find reason and logic in our lives and find some form of deeper meaning, when in reality there is rarely any deeper meaning to the events that have transcribed. Often more painful than the actual event is the time and effort we expend painfully trying to find meaning, which is akin to pouring salt on our own wounds as we ad nauseum repeat the experiences of the past in our minds to find some sense of normalcy or logic.

I found one of the most paramount reasons we are left in this perpetually abusive cycle of self-abuse is that we are often unable to differentiate our failures and adversities from our inner sense of self. We end up internalizing our failures from our point of view, and it takes an inexplicable amount of time, patience, and healing to get out of this vicious cycle. In essence, due to an absence of being able to protect ourselves from our thoughts, we become our failures, and in doing so we allow external, often unpredictable events to go ahead and dictate our internal, predictable environment. It is not uncommon to hear that our interpretation of events dictates our responses, and the key to an effective, efficient, and resilient recovery is the ability to transcend the act of failure from its key elements and separate them from internalizing the failure.

In essence, we need to clearly understand that we are not our failures; the fact that we have failed in one element in life does not in any way reflect the fact that we ourselves have become failures. Within each failure is a great opportunity for us to learn and move forward; however, that requires us to go beyond the emotional aspect of failure and fundamentally isolate our emotions to identify the learning opportunities presented before us. It is no secret that in any facet of life, the so-called experts in any field or profession have failed on far more numerous occasions than most average people have even attempted. But that transition in mentality is extremely difficult because our ego is hurt, and furthermore our focus has become external, so often we are more worried about how others will feel about our failures than ourselves.

Having sustained my fair share of failures, I realized that the only way to move forward is to painfully understand that my failures are only my failures, and that they are my sole property. The comments and criticisms of others do not in any way reflect meaningfully on my failure, since the locus of control has now been shifted from an internal focus to an external one. That shift in the locus of control is the quintessential reason whereby we misinterpret our failures instead of being great opportunities to learn. We view them as a source of shame, fear, or guilt. In taking ownership of our failures, we own them, and in a sense desensitize ourselves from the fact that we failed, which can allow our analytical sense to look into why it is we actually failed and how we can work on learning from this experience. That sounds far easier said than done; in order to actually be objective about our failures, we have to come to terms with who we are as individuals, and realize that in deconstructing our failures we are actually constructing our true selves. For it is in our moments of despair and weakness that we find out who we truly are, and we can use these opportunities to fill the gaps for a better sense of self. However, no matter how great the opportunity to learn may be from our failure, nothing will arise if we simply cannot let go of the fact that failure is a blessing in disguise.

One must also note that although it is imperative to overcome the fear of failure, like most things in life moderation is key. We cannot confuse our repeated failures without actionable changes in our patterns as being constructive. In the words of Albert Einstein, "The definition of insanity is doing the same thing over and over and expecting different results."

We have to disengage from the situation and interpret the results, almost as if we were to give advice to someone else. This is important, for we all know that we give the greatest advice to others; however, when it comes to ourselves, we forget all common sense and do exactly the opposite of what we have so sagely advised others. It is our analysis that bears the fruit of our misfortunes, and it is within that analysis we find ourselves and learn to avoid repeating the path that led to our failure. Failure is not an end result, but rather a part of a larger process, whereby we sharpen our skills, our thoughts, and our actions in order to create and embolden a wiser, smarter self.

ON LOSING MONEY

Today is the unfortunate day that I lost the majority of my savings on one single stock, an unproven, unverified, small penny stock company. To make matters worse, this same week I received some unfortunate news about my health a day before this stock crashed. I am still at an overwhelming loss as to how someone who built a business from ground up into a seven-figure business, and sold it at a good profit, could risk it all on a simple unproven stock in the anticipation of great rewards. How could someone give his life to create such a thriving business and sell it only to lose years of hard work in a flash of an instant in a stock?

Now of course, it's easy to go on and say you should have diversified, you should only risk what you can lose, and so on. However, this phenomenon is more common than you would imagine, and I can only delve into my own psyche to understand this week of all weeks. Let's call it black Wednesday.

These are some very good questions, and they relate to a deeper question of mis-matched priorities: why is it that someone chasing something almost never seems to receive what that they want? Easy money is one of the most common and underlying themes that relates to a lot of human beings who have committed such a sin. Rare is the person who can stay disciplined as a monk, sticking to common sense investing methodologies, that albeit boring are time tested, proven to preserve their capital, and provide long term gains with patience and cautiousness.

I will tell you why knowing all of these time proven principles, seasoned investors can sometimes go all in chasing the proverbial unicorn stock. The reason is quite simple: earning money through our employment and business is difficult, time consuming, and comes at a high emotional and physical cost. We all want that hit, that feeling of euphoria, and like most other vices, the longer you go without a victory, the more that burning desire is incensed. Like inebriated college students at our first spring party, we are excited by temptation without a second glance at the series of poor decisions we are about to commit for the sake of a good time. Well unfortunately, the most beautiful and rewarding things in life take time, patience, and commitment, and the reward is comparative to the care and time provided to the investment in these activities, such as relationships and business. Why is it that intelligent, conscientious investors can fall off the wagon and get sucked into this vortex of greed and easy money?

The reason being like most get rich schemes, for every winner there are a thousand losers. It goes without saying we automatically assume the other ninety- nine percent will be losers, and somehow with some magical beans we can be the proverbial golden ticket holder. Well, as I found out the hard way, if you walk into a room of investors and you can't find the sucker, you are the sucker. Yes, a very harsh truth, and today that was hammered into me so deeply and painfully, for a minute my concerns about my health were selfishly overridden by my ego, the same ego that guided me to leverage all my money on a silly stupid play. I have no one to blame but myself; everything was lined up for this to fly to the moon, and yet it didn't.

A series of black swan events transpired, which I am not sure if that term is relevant if you have many within a short period of time. I think at that time, the better expression would be shit out of luck. Henceforth, I was left in utter devastation that the majority of my life savings had been wiped out in an instant, and quite literally there was no one to blame other than myself. Now failure is not final, and often it is at moments like these where we come to terms with our own vulnerability as humans, investors, and rational individuals. We come to terms with the fact that the green devil of greed and jealousy is a sleeping giant within all of us, and when given the right stimuli can be aroused and guide us into utter devastation.

I realized that for me, this green devil I was not able to keep at bay led me into the utter destruction of my financial equity so unceremoniously, if I think of all the fun things I could have done with the loss of that money, it blows my mind that I allowed this to happen. After some deep soul searching, it has come to my realization that after suffering for so long fighting multiple cancer surgeries and chemo treatment, having been dealt with bad hand after bad hand, I placed a Hail Mary bet on something that deep down I knew was perhaps unwise. When we are down, we are told that eventually your day will come, we are taught to believe that eventually the bad luck will end. Well, I am here to inform you as a public service warning perhaps that is not always true; sometimes when you are kicked down again and again by life, the minute you raise your head, you are drop-kicked into the next week again.

Life is unrelenting, unforgiving, and sometimes when we are dealt with bad hands that we cannot fathom or comprehend, it places us in a deep, dark place, whereby we compound our troubles by grasping for straws, and end up short and shit out of luck.

Like most investors in my position, I am deeply disappointed in myself, but I realise what is more disappointing is instead of focusing on my health, I am focusing and chasing the very thing that is undoubtedly making me less healthy. One has to learn from one's mistakes, and today I learned a very poignant lesson about mismatched priorities and the importance of discipline and tempering greed.

Fortunately, there is no shortage of individuals that have been on the ropes financially and have rebounded strong. We have all learned lessons the hard way, and failure is never final. My focus has transitioned to care about my health and well-being, and I will focus on staying strong for myself and my family as I position myself to face the next round of challenges coming towards me, and staying strong through adversity. Sometimes in our most challenging and difficult of times, we look back fondly as they are marked as defining moments in our lives. Today is a defining moment for me, and although today is a very painful day, someday the lessons I will learn will pay multiples forward, not only financially, but also emotionally.

ON BEING INDESTRUCTIBLE

Have you ever wondered in life how some people can survive the most horrific of events, bounce back, get pummeled by life repeatedly, and then remarkably bounce back? How is that these human rubber balls can withstand the most extreme of circumstances and bounce back as if nothing happened? Sure, they may be beaten, broken, and worn out at times, but their spirits are indomitable. It is a level of resiliency and strength that comes from deep within. It is this innate battery that helps these individuals power through the most challenging mental and physical situations, and rise to the occasion time and time again.

Who are these magical people, and how can we aspire to be like them? Are they really human? What kind of superpowers do they possess, and how can we replicate their durability? The answer you are looking for is not as easy as you may think; in order to be able to endure the most difficult hardships, it is important firstly not to magnify the difficulty of the situation. It is not uncommon to find individuals that are not resilient to magnify the amplitude of the perceived hurt they have received. Even when it is not real, they make it so. They take perceived insults and losses that are minor, or may even be imaginary, and create an illusion that they are more real than life itself. Often, this comes from an innate need for attention, a look at my sense of approach to life. By drawing attention to whatever their minor or cursory problems may be, they draw power from the significance given to them by this amplification of minor setbacks and problems.

Those that are resilient often are silent. The aforementioned strong and silent stereotype is no illusion; it is real. The reason is that in order to endure a great amount of pain and suffering, one needs to look beyond oneself and realize that truly this too shall pass. This does not mean that they suffer the actual pain any less, it simply means that instead of choosing to amplify the destructive effects of the pain, they silently dissipate it. Coping mechanisms can vary and each individual has their own, but in my opinion the greatest ability to endure pain is to look it square in the eye and choose not to avoid it. It is the courage to stare our adversary head on which is, in my opinion, the single most determining factor in deciding if that individual will continue to cope well with adversity. The other most poignant factor is the ability to not make things worse than they are, and in order to do that, we almost need an out of body experience to step back and truly have a grander scope. It is important to realize that whatever may happen to us, often it is not fair and rarely is it so significant that we cannot overcome our adversity.

Often, it is no coincidence that a lot of the pain we endure in life comes from self-inflicted pain, be it bad habits or poor choices we repeat, not learning from our mistakes, doubling down on our mistakes, and so on. It is this self-inflicting nature of ourselves that we often find once we are knee-deep in misery, how we allowed this to come to fruition. The reason I bring up the self-inflicted nature of our pain is to illuminate the fact that it is not necessary to continuously suffer, and often it is in our best interest to do what we can to minimize that suffering. Life itself has no shortages of surprises up its sleeve, so why is it that so many of us cannot resist the opportunity to add to that can of worms. It is absolutely okay to make mistakes; however, it is even more important to identify how it is we made those mistakes and look for repeating patterns. The harder we look, the easier this will get. However, this process of self-discovery will have no fruition if we cannot get past the idea that we are incapable of making mistakes. In an ironic twist, the harder we try to fool ourselves that we are infallible, the more likely we are to fail and continue to suffer. I have come to terms with that sense of ego a long time ago; at this point I have no shame in admitting my failures and almost laughing at them. This process of letting go has not only allowed me to weather self-induced storms, but in addition, it has allowed me to gain access to key notes of wisdom from people around me.

The act of self-admission of failure is so rare, the act of humility so scarce, it is impossible for it not to attract the admiration and respect of those around that truly care. The reason it is so inspiring is that it takes a tremendous amount of courage to admit that we have failed, and the mere act of doing so is akin to unlocking an alternate universe of guilt-free mental peace. So much of our mental anxiety is from failure to admit our mistakes, especially to loved ones, for the simple act that we are bracing for the lecture or scolding to follow. After several repeated patterns of behaviour, this becomes ingrained in our modus operandi, and we are destined to act accordingly in other situations whereby we may be embarrassed by our actions. The irony of all this is when facing circumstances where our adversity is self-imposed, our secret weapon is self-admission and self-study in order to minimize the devastating effects of our actions.

Now life, on the other hand, cares not how hard we are actively trying to sabotage ourselves; life has its own swiss army knife of problems, and as soon as we are out of one, it has no problems throwing a few more curveballs down our way for no reason whatsoever. I think the hardest time that anyone has in attempting to be resilient against life's constant barrages is that often life is unpredictable, illogical, and unfair. It is in our culture and nature to try to make logical sense of an illogical world. Why do certain devastating events only happen to some people? How can other nefarious characters continually get away with illicit behaviour? How are some people so seemingly lucky, and others cursed? It is this illogical and unpredictable behaviour of life that makes it difficult for us to train to be resilient, the very simple reason being that it is very difficult to prepare if our focus is on the outwards world. As you know, the outside world is unpredictable and violently volatile; however, it is our inner world where we find peace. It is in our inner sense of calm that we breathe and find some rationale as to how to proceed forwards.

So how does one deal with this unpredictable, irrational, and most certainly unfair world? I think the simplest answer that I have found that helps me deal with devastating setback after setback is the fact that I refused to listen to the self-depreciating narrative that starts with "why me?" Once we delve into the why me, we follow with the comparison to others, and then we come up with a checklist of our good deeds and compare them to people around us that are perhaps not as noble, yet seemingly untouched by life. Therein starts a vortex of mental despair that is hard to escape; the more we want not to think about it, the more we get swept up into it. We fall into dark thoughts, enter scary areas whereby we are unable to process not only our devastating circumstances, but we compound this problem by comparison, and therein lies the trap. Call it the "why me" trap. I have found perhaps the best and simplest way is to isolate yourself from your mind, and have an out-of-body experience in order to better survey the challenges. Through crises come great opportunities, and the best way to take advantage of them is to embrace them rather than fight, spend less time wondering why me, and more time trying to understand how to fight, and what to do to make the best out of this. By transferring the mental energy from what we cannot control and what already has been done, rather than to what we can change and how we can take advantage of it, we shift the narrative. That is the secret sauce for those that embrace challenges and do not get caught in the victim mentality and make the best of the worst of situations even when facing something as dire as certain death.

So, in summary, when faced with adverse circumstances that may be in your control or may not be, the best advice I can provide, having faced life and death situations pertaining to my cancer, is to breathe and take it one day at a time. Life is often unpredictable, both good and bad, and when it is bad we often amplify the level of doom and make it worse. This helps no one and is akin to flailing your arms as you sink in quicksand. In order to escape the trap of self-depreciation and gloom, it is imperative to have an out-of-body experience and survey the best and worst case scenarios. Prepare for the worst, embrace your challenges, and slowly proceed to disseminate the information provided to you. The key is to embrace the lack of control instead of rallying against it; this not only saves your precious energy, but helps you focus in order to figure out your plan of attack. In this regard, the slow silent deliberation is far more effective and efficient than flamboyantly panicking to all those around us. It is no secret that those that have tremendous burdens to bear are so humble and courageous as they battle the most difficult battles alone, scared, and in pain, yet so strong that they silently endure in order to preserve a sense of order as their world falls apart. When reality is thrust into your face in such a black and white manner, it is easy to lose the self-induced illusions we may have falsely created when left with binary choices such as life or death. This new reality that is thrust upon us allows us to shed our previous illusions that may or may not be conceived vicariously, and we are allowed a blank slate to start afresh. Your mind will be allowed to start afresh, and it is the wisest amongst us that recognize this new beginning and embrace it, rather than fight it and be sent into the murky hells of a vortex of fear and despair. Fear not your future, for often it is out of your control. Do your best to make your short time in this hurt a little easier, for no one will do it for you, and no matter what happens, good or bad, embrace it with stoic nature, for you are not your failures and your misfortune should never define you.

INTERRUPTED THOUGHTS:
ON LUCK

What is luck, this paradigm that is blessed only upon some and not on others? This is a complicated subject, and often how we look at luck depends on our perspective of how much we may feel we have been blessed with it. This is an interesting concept, because so often we confuse years of hard work, dedication, and subsequent success as being merely a factor of luck. They say it's no coincidence that those who are dedicated and work diligently are naturally lucky in their endeavours. However, what about those individuals that have done all of the above?

ON PUPPIES

One of the most beautiful and lovable creatures on this planet is a puppy. Anyone who has ever had the pleasure of spending time with a puppy can only stand in awe and admiration of such a beautiful creature. This is not to take away from other animals, but it is more a testament to the beautiful, sweet, and gentle nature of such a kind animal. Now why, you ask, would I take the time to speak about puppies. We all know them as being cute, fluffy, and sometimes annoying, but despite all their mischievous behaviours, it is really hard not to love them. They are a small microcosm as to what our ideal selves could be, so pure of love and kindness. It is hard not to admire their spirit.

The reason I am speaking about puppies is that for the majority of my childhood and adulthood, I have always wished for a puppy, but raising a puppy is a great responsibility and my parents were strongly against the idea, so that did not help my aspirations. A few months after I had recovered from my first cancer treatment, I had this strong urge for companionship, and the unconditional, therapeutic love of a puppy is second to none. So, I decided that indeed I would go ahead and get my puppy. I went with my best friend to take a look at her, and it was truly love at first sight. I needed a friendly and calm breed that I could take to the clinic and eventually train as a therapy dog. Therapy not only for me, but for all my anxious patients and children that would come to the clinic, as the dentist is usually high up on most everyone's idea of the worst place imaginable to ever be at.

As winter fell upon us in the late days of November, I brought home the most beautiful labradoodle named Maya. She had the most beautiful red coat, and she stole my heart from the minute I set eyes upon her. Maya has been a fundamental part of my life ever since she graced me with her presence. Her pleasant, sweet-tempered nature has been instrumental in keeping my spirits up as I healed both mentally, physically, and emotionally from one of the most traumatic experiences of my life.

In my clinic, we found a home for baby Maya behind the front desk. My staff fell in love with her, and soon enough she was an integral part of the clinic. Patients would come in asking for her, she enjoyed lots of love from young children that would find her to be the highlight of their visit. In general, she left the clinic, and to a smaller extent the heart of everyone that visited her, just that much better. During my lunches, I would take her out for a walk every day, and this allowed me to enjoy peace and quality time with her. After a frenzied, hectic day, it provided me a moment of solitude and peace to calm my spirits as I enjoyed the exuberant enthusiasm baby Maya showed for the world around. There is something so fundamentally pure about the sheer love Maya demonstrated for everyone and everything around her left me in awe at her innocence and sweetness.

Perhaps the most remarkable aspect of having Maya was the way in which she slowly changed those around me. Her ever-present loving spirit even melted the hearts of my parents, who were strongly against ever having a dog. My mom, still heartbroken from the loss of her childhood dog, refused to ever allow another dog into the family. Her pretense was that dogs were a lot of work and hassle; the reality was that she was scared to love again, and due to the short life span of dogs, to endure another death. My father on the other hand was traumatized from childhood due to a poorly trained dog that attacked him. Despite how cuddly Maya was, he was petrified to even come close or be touched by her. Well, it is hilarious how the tides have turned, and my parents have so lovingly embraced Maya into their lives, sometimes it is suspect as to who the actual owners of the dog are. What used to be, "Have a good night Manu," soon turned into, "Goodnight Maya, sweet dreams." Conveniently, all the attention was on Maya, and honestly who can blame them. This wonderful change in attitude has provided my parents with great comfort and therapy during what can only be described as a tumultuous period of time.

Although Maya was not there with me during my first cancer treatment, she was by my side during my second surgery and chemoradiation. Dogs, they say, have a natural instinct to understand when something is amuck, and you could bear witness the sadness in her eyes as she knew something was wrong with her owner. Day after day, as I withstood the pain and suffering of the treatments, little Maya was by my side, providing me and my parents with great comfort and relief. It is in moments like these that we realize perhaps we are not worthy of animals; our own human nature is a convoluted mess of generally selfish and conflicting sets of behaviours and emotions. It is in moments like these where we realize that perhaps if there is a divine spirit, it is embedded within the souls of these gentle animals.

In summary, Maya has been a tremendous blessing upon us. She has helped my family overcome great grief and loss, and has given a renewed hope that life can indeed be pure and beautiful again. I am continuously in awe of her spirit and innocence that remind me perhaps there is a greater truth that our polluted minds, in all our human wants and needs, cannot seem to grasp. Perhaps there is a true divine energy that supersedes our petty needs and wants, and perhaps these animals serve as a gentle reminder to embrace that spirit and think beyond ourselves once in a while, as past our own limitations there is beauty.

ON PARENTS

Perhaps the greatest blessing that has been imparted upon me has been the love of my parents. They have throughout my life become the greatest source of strength, wisdom, inspiration, and love. I have learned so much through their wisdom; they have held me when they themselves were weak, and they have supported me when I deserved to be left to suffer by my own doings. Through infinite wisdom they have guided me through some truly bleak and miserable moments in my life, they have given me unconditional love, and for that I am truly grateful.

Now I understand everyone has a different relationship with their parents, and that not all of us are blessed with such loving and supportive relationships. Nevertheless, I would like to speak about my good fortune in this matter simply as a blessing that I am fully aware of and only increasingly aware as time passes me by. There are some of us who have not had such a blessed childhood, and have suffered based on poor choices imparted upon them by their parents. There are also others who have had some great blessings imparted upon them by their parents, but sometimes we can be so self-absorbed in our own world that we can take these for granted. Luckily, parents that truly care don't forget us, even though sometimes we can forget their value and wisdom in times of need.

I have always held a very confident view of the world, and I never for a minute discounted my future contributions to the world, partly because I always felt the blessings and support of my parents as an insurance policy. I felt that no matter how badly my ventures may fail, no matter how silly my misadventures may be, either financial or romantic, I felt like there was always a safety net. That safety net gave me unfound confidence that I felt I would not have had if I ignored the blessings of my parents. That sense of security in a world that is difficult, unpredictable, unfair, and downright scary at times is valuable beyond measure.

As a young adult, I felt my parents' fears about the world and their subsequent warnings about issues in finance, education, and relationships came from a position of fear. Perhaps I felt that way simply because as a brazen young adult with inexperience, I confused a defense- first strategy as a sign of weakness. I felt like most who have not waged war against a real world that is often unforgiving and rarely generous; that such a defense- first policy of caution and protecting yourself first as being grossly short-sighted and dripping in fear. In hindsight, as years have gone on and I have battled life's unpredictable and unforgiving journey, I realize that those fears were not due to weakness, but warnings given from a vantage point experience. Those astute warnings about the dangers to be wary of were not from a position of weakness, but rather a gift of wisdom through sheer love and thoughtfulness, such that I may not suffer.

Perhaps nothing sums up the fallacy of our human nature better than Will Rogers when he states, "There are three kinds of men. The ones that learn by reading'. The few who learn by observation. The rest of them have to pee on the electric fence for themselves." As someone who is a self-professed idiot in choosing option number three a lot, and peed on far too many electric fences, I have become tired and weary of option number three. Having realized that my body and mind can only take so much abuse, I have come to terms with my own fallacies, and have chosen to realize that perhaps there is a better way. Perhaps if I let my ego take a well-deserved rest, there is wisdom to some of the snippets of advice my parents have been giving me for free for a lifetime it seems.

We are such funny creatures sometimes that when we are tired of peeing on fences, we would rather spend untold fortunes on self-help guides and inspirational seminars, rather than simply revisit the patient and kind advice our elders have been trying to give us. We would rather spend money to hear the almost ubiquitous truths about life and wisdom and take a flight to a seminar, only to hear someone who is making obscene amounts of wealth by simply recycling and regurgitating truths that have existed for centuries. It would be simply beneath us to take some time out of our day and listen to the struggles of our parents and the subsequent wisdom gained from them in order to learn these very lessons in life.

Often our parents are humble and gracious in their accomplishments and difficulties they may have endured simply to sustain you and your precious childhood. They are often either embarrassed by their own difficulties, or would rather choose not to tarnish your version of your childhood with inconvenient truths about the actual realities they faced. It is in these glossed over or unspoken realities that we can find infinite wisdom. Wisdom that is free, wisdom that is true, wisdom that is real and time tested. It is in our prerogative to move past our egos and explore these truths from people that have faced the wrath of time and survived again and again.

Now I understand that not everyone holds such a close and amiable relationship with their parents, but surely there are individuals in your life that are older, wiser, and have time- tested strategies that have endured. Wisdom is all around us; often we ignore it in the sense that if you are like me, your arrogance and ego prevent you from stooping so low as to be bothered to ask for such help. Why? For you are a young stallion, setting out upon a world that is yours to conquer; there is no alternate plan for you because victory is imminent, and quite frankly almost a given for you. After some failures in life which are also a given, as no one in any position of success in any field has not endured a multitude of failures before achieving anything, you realize that not only is victory not a given, but in fact surviving to fight another day is imperative.

It is no secret that youth is wasted upon the young, and that wisdom is only imparted upon us after we have peed on one too many electric fences to learn invaluable lessons that our egos would otherwise prevent us from learning. We realize that in order to succeed in life, it is important to have a safety-first mentality, as it is imperative to withdraw from a bloody battlefield to live and fight another day, rather than to lay it all on the line and be left with nothing. There are rarely second chances; life is not some video game we can respawn, nor are we corporate panhandlers that after unforgivable financial mistakes as corporations often do, we receive a generous bailout that allows us to continue our stupidity till the next bailout. No siree, life is not so kind for the individual, often there are no second plans, and no one is there for your bailout, other than perhaps your parents. Not perhaps because they are keen to do so, but the bonds of love move past our egos and make sure we take care of our loved ones.

It is our duty not to abuse these bonds of love if you are so lucky as to have them in the first place. The love of your parents knows no bounds; often it is abused or ignored until we are in a position for a bailout. All I am asking is before you are in dire circumstances, take the time to acknowledge and appreciate the wisdom around you. Set your ego aside before it is too late, and take some time to inherit more than just genetics. Your parents may have struggled far more than you know, and often it is their unconditional love that prevents them from ever mentioning you as a burden. All that

I would ask, regardless of age, is that the next time they lecture you on life, maybe just maybe, instead of rolling your eyes, perhaps take out a pen and paper, as it might save your hide someday.

ON MORTALITY

I find perhaps one of the most intriguing aspects about our fears regarding mortality is those who have never even come close to facing their own mortality are the most fearful of it. For those of us who have come close to death and have had to face our own fears head on, we almost become desensitized to the concept. In my personal opinion, the reason is that as a concept of our imagination, the fear of death and leaving this earth is far more powerful as an illusion than it is as an actual reality.

It is far easier to create this grandiose concept regarding our mortality as some powerful event, that we need to delay and prolong its eventual execution. It is in our own delusions that we feel we have some massive contribution yet to provide to this earth. However, if we did not feel that our mortality is near, would we be so inclined to create such a magnificent vision of our yet-to-be contributions? If we were so inclined to provide such a magnificent contribution to humankind, would we not have started this journey far earlier? The more sober reality, once you have faced your own mortality, is that death is often non-discriminatory in nature; it cares not about your grandiose plans, and is often humiliating and sudden in nature, a non-event if you will. In a moment, we are here on this earth, alive, breathing, and in a moment we are not. We are silent, still, and all those dreams, illusions, thoughts, visions disappear with us, or do they?

If our time on this earth is finite, and our visions and dreams infinite, how can we face our mortality and translate it into something that will extend beyond our mere mortal body? Is it possible to translate our visions and thoughts beyond eternity? Is it possible that the solution to our fears of mortality is to transcend beyond the superficial and extend into a reality that is entrenched in our own truth? A truth so strong that it will speak to generations centuries after we have long left this earth?

In my own personal view, having faced death on multiple occasions, it has become clear to me that my own mortality has transcended as being from a far-fetched distant concept, and descended into an everyday reality. I no longer attempt to escape this very real possibility, yet instead I have chosen to embrace it wholeheartedly with the familiarity and constant presence of an old friend. It is a reminder of my fragility, however, rather than a source of fear and stress. It is an ever-present reminder to find my true purpose.

If my death is ever-present and predetermined, but my possibilities are infinite, should I not focus on translating whatever finite time I may have on this earth into a more real possibility? How much of our true potential is lost on a daily basis by our getting sucked into a vortex of the mundane and routine? If we were able to accurately get an estimate as to the exact time and date on which we were to die, how would our behaviours and actions change on a daily basis? The reason I am asking all these questions is that I am most certainly guilty of wasting years of my talent and aspirations in the pursuit of more mundane themes of materialism, and fulfilling basic human desires never aspiring beyond my own selfish themes.

With a newfound sense of familiarity with my mortality, I have come to the conclusion that it is a far more purposeful and useful pursuit to provide service to our fellow humans than it is to be immortal. It is in the hope that our actions and thoughts for the betterment of others would remain eternal, that we should try to focus not on our finite mortality, but on our infinite potential. Ironically, it is in finding your purpose that we can provide the most reasonable way for our thoughts and actions to remain eternal.

One of the interesting dualities of the modern world is that technology and access to the internet has delivered us immediate results. However, in that sense of speed we have lost sight of the meaning of time. What I mean is that we seek immediate satisfaction and immediate results, and seek methods to validate our sense of position within the world with forms of trophies as measures of success. Yet ironically, in that sense mortality respects no timeline or carefully conceived image projected on social media. Without original thoughts and ideas, the idea of an influencer is not original in its nature; we all seek meaning and validation through the approval of others. What is interesting to note is that ironically, the wisdom of those who have long since passed has transcended centuries and civilizations to leave us with their ever-relevant wisdom. They have found immortality by providing benefit to their common man; they did not seek to exploit them for monetary gains or social standing based on followers. Often, they were simply attempting to seek some universal truths, and it is in their discoveries that they have found true immortality.

So in summary, what I have noted is that death is not a final destination that we slowly descend into after we have accomplished all that we set out to do so in an orderly fashion. No, the concept of our mortality is an ever-present factor of our life. Death, if you will, follows you at every step and at every hour, you cannot escape it. Perhaps, the best manner in which to cope with this reality is to embrace it rather than remain in fear of it, for your thoughts will not change the reality of how our lives proceed.

What we can do, however, is to give the concept of our mortality the respect it deserves, and translate that into a quest to provide a sense of fulfillment in our daily lives, and perhaps the most fruitful path to fulfillment is to provide valuable service to others.

Now I am not asking us all to immediately become saintly in our daily lives, but merely suggesting that we start by slowly thinking beyond the self-absorbed sphere that we are so often caught up in. By providing thoughts and ideas that we hope to outlive us, we can start work towards creating our own solution for our mortality. That solution is that in creating something of value that will outlast us, we will in essence take the first step of immortality, and that alone is our only hedge against the fear of mortality. Our lives will come and go, but our ideas will remain immortal, and therefore in essence the soul behind our work remains eternal. So, seek not to fear your own mortality, but rather embrace the challenge to create something that will outlive your fears and wildest imaginations, such that you may be able to provide service years after you have dearly departed. Live with the strength that not only is this not impossible, but quite tangible if we can simply let go of fears that will not serve us any purpose in this life or the next.

ON FINDING
INTERNAL PEACE

On a daily basis in our modern world, we are bombarded with an overwhelmingly diverse number of distractions and stimuli. Should we even attempt to evade them, the fact that the rest of the world is perpetually hooked on them places us in a distinct social disadvantage. We can elicit anger and resentment should we not answer to these daily calls, when in fact the world has seemingly confused what is immediate with what is important. However, sometimes we are blessed with opportunities where we are forced without our consent to stop, and subsequently discover that if we come to a halt, our world will carry on.

Nothing brings one's world crashing to a halt more than when you are stripped of all your stimuli, and lie half naked in an awkwardly fitting patient gown on a hospital bed, staring out through a window into a world that you may not currently be allowed to participate in. Nothing brings one's ego to a halt more when none of your accomplishments, degrees, or status matters, as you lie there waiting, sometimes hours on end, as your life rests in the balance of physicians and nurses. As you lie stationary, sometimes for hours in numbing silence, you start to realize that nothing of what you perceive really matters. We are all constructs of our own self-importance, and ironically none of that really matters when it counts most, especially as in my case, as cancer cells continue to destroy one's own body with no reasoning and with reckless abandon.

We often try socially to impart our importance on to others, yet the irony of the fact is that it was a fruitless effort, evidenced most when you sit there helpless, temporarily displaced from your world in a form of time warp. Nothing matters at this moment; none of your trivial daily tasks matter, as you are stripped of all ego and left in a meditative state. Often, we find this meditative state hard to reach during our busy lives, and it requires great practice and patience to reach such a state.

As we lie in a hospital, often alone, afraid, in pain, and deeply scared, a sense of calm starts to overwhelm us. That calm, in my case, was from the realization that whatever has happened has happened, and whatever my future will be it is beyond my immediate control. And alas, as that responsibility towards my future was relieved, a great peacefulness overcame me as I endured difficult procedure after procedure, multiple tests, pain, silence, and loneliness. I became my greatest advocate; often the same mind that would criticize me for mistakes made and opportunities lost became my most compassionate friend, and advocate for inner peace. In a sense, I forgave myself for mistakes past, present and future.

I experienced many out-of-body experiences as I allowed my mind to escape itself, and almost witnessed as a third party the horrors the physical body was experiencing. I realized the only way in which I would escape without anger, regret, or fear would be to embrace all that is happening to me and never question why. I found myself escaping to a happier place, a place of calm and peace, as the physical body endured torture after torture. This is not an easy practice, but by mentally separating my time and space from the present into a more pleasant and rewarding mental place, it allowed me temporary relief. I am by no means a spiritual master, nor have I practiced many of these spiritual forms of meditation and self-awareness during my daily routines. Yet, when times were most dire, my body automatically withdrew into this meditative state of peace and happiness as I separated the unfortunate reality of the present with the pleasant thoughts I escaped to within my mind. All the attributes of daydreaming that as a student I was reprimanded for, as an adult fighting for my life, I was rewarded greatly.

If there ever was a gift from all my struggles, it was the idea of priorities and principles. What I mean to say is that activities we may have considered in passing as trivialities became lifesaving habits and ideas, and the practices we considered as essential were, in fact, self-destructive nuisances. Of all things, I learned to smile and endure during the worst of times, because I realized for the first time the lack of control, and instead of fighting it, I embraced it. It gave me so much freedom to let go of the selfish ego, and go along for the journey. It allowed me to not only escape the pain, but also to engage in an unbiased manner the lessons given to me daily, as my fate was beyond my control. Of course, I did my best to help my body fight in terms of diet, exercise, and basic tenets that one should do when facing life threatening diseases. However, perhaps my greatest victory was to let go and internally smile in solitude as I detached from my intense reality and entered into a more peaceful and meditative state.

The greatest lesson imparted to me is that we are far greater than the physical state of our body; our mind is a separate entity in and of itself. When we allow the mind to supersede the immediate demands of the body, we can find a most wonderful place that protects us from self-injury. As long as the mind can endure and be protected, the body will soon follow. We are far more capable and resilient than we can begin to imagine. For once, I focused not on external states, but on internal states of resilience, calm, and forgiveness, and in doing so I found peace. I did not find my peace because I was comfortable, but because in my most extreme states of discomfort, I found a place so beautiful, so calm, and so serene, and that most magical place was my mind.

ON TROPHIES

Have you ever stopped to wonder why society has such an intense love affair with trophies? These shiny medallions of our achievements have long transcended civilisations as testaments to victory and success. What is it about these items of great symbolic value that makes us work with dogged determination to acquire them? Why are we so determined to simply hold these items, that in themselves have no intrinsic value, other than the fact that they serve as a reminder that to the victor shall go the spoils. What is it in our competitive nature that as a civilization, we require cooperation to survive evolutionarily, yet in the same breath we strive to asymmetrically reward competition?

As a young man, I collected a great many of these trophies. They were the pinnacle of my achievements, and provided me with a great sense of pride and ego in terms of my accomplishments. More so than me, it provided my parents with a great sense of satisfaction and pride that perhaps surpassed even mine. As I got older, and arguably somewhat wiser, I realized these trophies and medallions slowly disappeared, and were replaced with what I would like to call "adult trophies." The adult trophies we collect as we age can be far more diverse than the trophies of our youth.

These can range a spectrum to include anything and everything, from exotic cars, houses to even trophy wives or husbands.

One would think that as a society evolves over centuries, there would be some form of sophistication in terms of favouring a more cooperative approach. Ironically, as we evolve as a society there is a greater and greater tendency to compete. Unlike previous generations, where there was genuinely a need to compete for limited resources, in today's developed society where for the most part the basic elements of survival, food, and shelter are covered, these trophies are coveted for the sake of collection.

After a certain point in life, for those of us who are able to accumulate enough to satisfy most of our basic needs for food and safety, there is an almost insatiable desire stoked by the ever presence of advertising and media to collect more trophies and proudly display them. Without an internal source of peace and calm, we are more inclined to be swayed by these daily influencing factors to display our suggested status as winners in life. I have on more than one occasion been influenced by this desire to establish an unnecessary need for these trophies. I would find a multitude of ways to justify the need for a bigger house, a nicer car, and so on, in an endless array of self-delusion that would sometimes use the pain of the past to justify pleasure in the present. Now, I am not suggesting that we all take a minimalist approach to life, but what I have discovered is that sometimes, we need to take a closer look into our own motivations and isolate if those thoughts are actually ours.

With the advent of social media, and a society perpetually connected online, we are influenced by so many factors that constantly pinge on our attention. Without a form of meditation, we can unknowingly be drawn into a state of mind that may not be authentically ours. Have you ever stopped to wonder if things that you naturally assumed to be your goals and aims were actually yours? Sometimes if we step back, we can find in so many factors that many of the thoughts and ideas we presumed to be the natural order of things were not even ours to begin with. We will advocate for these thoughts and set upon our journeys to achieve them, and if we are fortunate enough one day, we will come to the shock realization that perhaps what we thought was so clear and natural was simply an illusion.

Perhaps one of the fastest, yet most difficult ways to step out of this illusion is to endure loss in life. This could be loss of health, status, occupation, and so on. It is a systemic shock to your natural order of things, and it removes away the superficial layers of fluff until you are left with a raw perspective of what is real and what is important. It is at this moment, like a lightning rod, it hits you that perhaps much of what you thought of as normal and orderly was actually never so, and what you thought was the way was never meant to be your way in the first place.

It is said that when we lose our senses in one aspect, the body compensates by heightening our other senses. Similarly, I would like to propose the idea that as we lose a sense of our identity in one aspect, we quickly adapt to compensate with other parts of our being in order to find balance. For example, when due to my health concerns I was forced to leave my occupation and let go of my business, I transferred that sense of being into another realm. I found that as I let go of the prototypical idea of being a successful doctor and business owner, and embraced writing as a release of my true creative talents, I found my inner identity flow into another sphere. I am no less successful or capable than before, but life has found a unique way to guide me to channel my energies into perhaps my true being.

There are no right answers to life, but I found as I was slowly stripped of my health, my status as an active doctor, and a successful businessman, I emerged to find my true identity. I found myself transferring away from seeking trophies and spending the time to appreciate small things, such as the beauty in my surroundings, the love of my parents, the support of my friends, and new passions and hobbies that had little fiscal reward, but were priceless for my soul. I have no doubt that as I heal I will someday re-enter the arena that is our society as a productive member, but what is unique is that I will no longer seek these trophies as means of accomplishment, but rather ask my truer self what is necessary, and what is truly meaningful.

Now this has been my personal journey and reflection. If you have found your true self years ago, then you have my deepest respect. It is not easy to navigate the rapidly changing constructs of our society, and most of us are naturally competitive, so it is even harder to just walk away from the race and simply go enjoy the sunshine while we are alive. If there is something that you must seek, and that you would be equally content with no one knowing about it, then you have truly found something of meaning that you should cherish. These words I write are a means to heal my own soul, and I would be just as content if they were typed up and left for no one to see than if they were printed and published. I have found my soul, and there is no trophy in the world for that accomplishment.

ON THE BEAUTY
OF SMALL THINGS

I used to feel that in order to appreciate true beauty in the universe, one has to view things in a grand scale, that the magnitude of the event would translate into something far grander than us. However, over time I have come to appreciate that some of the most beautiful things in life are on a smaller scale, and that often due to their size they are underappreciated and overlooked. There is great sophistication in simplicity, and as we come to gain a better appreciation of our place in life over the years, we start to appreciate the simpler, and ultimately more beautiful things in life. The reason being is that as children, we experience pure joy in the simplicity of life, yet as we grow older that simplicity is undermined, and we slowly evolve into complicating our lives as a natural progression.

It is our folly as we grow older that we will act in disdain when something is not grandiose and magnificent, and discount it as such. However, the simple joys that we experienced as children, unknown to our older, unwise selves, were the ultimate expressions of beauty. Often in our haste to rush through our lives in working towards larger, grand master plans scheduled out in neat time increments, we forget that the destination is irrelevant, and it is the journey that matters. During this journey, in our haste to get through our days, hours, and minutes, we overlook the small things around us and fail to appreciate how truly beautiful they are. We would rather sit and complain about things not going according to our plans that have no guarantee, since life has no master, rather than appreciate the beauty around us.

Sometimes when simple things are taken away, only then do you start to appreciate the beauty that for so long you have overlooked. It is often our folly that only when things are taken from us do we start to get a true learned experience of how things we perceived as being simple and unmentionable were actually part of a beautiful orchestra. As individual elements start to fall apart, only then do we see past the illusion of the mundane and boring, and get a true grasp as to just how beautiful simplicity truly was.

To give you an example that may make this concept more relatable, let us take a look at the simple art of breathing. On a daily basis, this may seem simple and mundane to us, but it involves complex physiological processes. We don't appreciate these processes until we are dealt with ill health, and breathing becomes difficult. I have experienced what it is like to have persistent shortness of breath as a consequence of my cancer, where simple activities became difficult and restful sleep was but a dream in itself. When taking a breath itself became difficult, all else rarely mattered, something that most of us take for granted, yet when taken away can shake the foundations of your being. I do not wish this state upon anyone, even for the remarkable lessons it may teach you, but I would rather you take the time at this moment to appreciate all that you have.

It is this irony that we often don't value things till they are taken away. That is such a perverse dichotomy; we seek things that when they are in our midst lose value, and the most valuable and beautiful things in life we ignore until they are taken away. The human mind can be so self-detrimental, we can often remain in a distant place, ignoring our immediate surroundings in search of a presumably better place. The irony of all this is that when we do reach these places or people, we have convinced ourselves in our minds we are often disappointed, and we find fault in them and choose instead to long for something better. This vicious cycle plagues many of us, and the reality of the situation comes from an inability to appreciate the present moment. Subsequently, we also discount many of the beautiful actions being performed around us in search of some greater truth that may never exist.

Life teaches us many lessons; it is our duty as the student to choose whether or not we wish to digest these lessons. As I stand as a passive observer of my own journey as my life has been spun into an incomprehensible turmoil, I find myself almost bemused by my ignorance in my earlier years. As simple things were slowly taken away from me, I began to truly appreciate their value, and it is sad that it took to this level of loss to understand true value, but I am grateful that I could take something meaningful from this.

Life is beautiful in all its elements, simple and complex. It should be our duty to truly appreciate the simple moments, because you will find that they will be the first to be taken away, and you will find their loss the most significant. It's what you never saw coming that will bring you to your knees, and in that moment of temporary weakness, you truly appreciate how beautiful that element of life truly was. As an ever-present student of life, I take these new lessons with gratefulness, for they have forever changed me. I do not view loss as suffering, but rather as the difficult work required to gain a deeper understanding of the energies that fuel our very being as an element of this universe.

ON BEAUTIFUL SOULS

Have you ever come across people whose souls are absolutely beautiful, their eternal sunshine beams an intense radiance when you are in their presence? The most beautiful souls that we will ever come across in our life are rarely born that way. The truth is that the most beautiful souls that we come across in our life have endured far more suffering than we can begin to imagine. The beauty in their souls arises not from our superficial versions of what beauty may be, but rather from taking the idea of grief that we often look upon in fear and distress, and finding a way to make even grief a beautiful part of life.

In a sense, these beautiful souls amongst us are an ever-present reminder that life is precious and fragile, and that circumstances can toughen us. However, we cannot allow these events in our lives to make us so rigid that we may never love again, that we may never be soft enough again to embrace the vivid energy that is life. Often, we take grief as a sign of weakness and tragedy. What if our grief was not the tragedy we made it out to be, but rather a lifeblood of both learning and renewal in life?

It is often our human nature to view tragic events as setbacks, but what if these events are merely signs of new beginnings, events that will ultimately result in happiness depending on our views of them? The beautiful souls among us have a remarkably different perspective to our often-scarce view of life, for if one's soul has mastered itself, it will remain eternal. Our physical beings are here for a finite amount of time; how finite will depend on many factors, but often it is out of our control. In order to remain eternal, our soul has to be transcribed into something that will outlive our physical being.

I have wrestled with these thoughts as I ask myself, what would constitute a life well lived? Would one rather live a shorter, more fulfilled life, or a longer, more miserable one? What would be truer to our eternal souls? These are some difficult questions, and quite frankly, I don't believe that there is any good answer to them. I feel the best way we can live our best lives is to engulf the lessons around us, and sometimes a multitude of those lessons can be found near us within these beautiful souls.

There are many beautiful souls that have encountered so much resistance and misfortune, it may seem their whole life has been rigged against them. While others may easily sail through the passages of life, these beautiful souls are sentenced to seemingly endless misery and suffering. Now here is the beautiful part: it is these beautiful, troubled souls that find the true meaning of happiness, since they are not gifted with easy circumstances. They find the true meaning of life through these difficult circumstances. You will also see many people gifted with endless luxuries and easy passages through life drowning in narcissistic angst of depression and self-hate that is not surprisingly of their own doing.

I feel that the key factor here is the matter of choice in circumstances. Often, the most beautiful of souls are not given a choice as to their misfortune, they are simply bombarded with one unfortunate event after another. These beautiful souls are good people, have been kind throughout their lives, and in no way do they deserve any of what is served to them in the platter of life. Yet, what makes these souls so beautiful is they do not reside permanently in their own anger, and they do not plead with the heavens above as to why they of all people were cursed as such.

These beautiful souls are blessed with a sense of resiliency and stoicism that transcends such petty insults to egos, and that is why it is no surprise the people around are the most affected when these individuals are cursed with misfortune. As one adapts to the chaos that descends when life happens, one begins to develop a deep sense of self-love and pure resilience that inherently protects them. By releasing themselves from petty ego centric emotions such as anger, comparison, and jealousy, they can transcend beyond what is destroying their lives and find peace amongst chaos. They can make jokes in the direst of circumstances, as they rarely take life so seriously, the reason being is that life happens, good or bad, and being serious only removes the joy out of moments that need not be so.

You see these beautiful souls, who are constantly faced with limited choices in their lives due to circumstances beyond them, begin to enjoy these limited choices even more, and appreciate the fact that there is even a choice. Those of us blessed with far too many options in life often lose the value of individual options ,and what should be a fortunate event to be able to choose simply morphs into a nuisance. That is the power of having more limited outlooks and more limited choices; it in fact drives more happiness than less as you appreciate that you even have a choice in the matter, and the selection carries more weight.

So much of what we appreciate in modern society is contrary to the lessons imparted upon us by these beautiful souls. It is a shame that these brilliant outlooks rarely see the light of day as we all chase the plethora of meaningless choices we have created for ourselves. You can see this from the fact that as we are blessed with so much opportunity and choice in this modern era, depression and anxiety are increasing at alarming rates.

I will explain what I have come to appreciate as life has led me into misfortune after misfortune, and that is it has made life so simple, and in that I have found much peace. I do not have many choices; it is either to live or die, to survive and fight another day or to pass into an eternal slumber. This makes life easy, for I appreciate every day, I appreciate every fight, and I am no longer dragged in a multitude of superfluous, meaningless options that drag me in a multitude of directions. In tragedy, I have found optimism and peace, I have enjoyed my days of utter simplicity, and I appreciate the most mundane and simple choices, as I still have the beautiful capacity to make those choices. Many have come before me, and many will come after me. I am not special, but my soul may remain eternal, as it will always be beautiful, and it was tragedy that made it so. For that, I am truly appreciative.

ON NEW BEGINNINGS

One of the most important things in life is to understand that failure is not final, we may fail time and time again, and our failures do not define us. We do not become our failures; there is not an individual that has accomplished anything of substance that has not failed time and time again. Failure is a natural part of life, and it is our ability to understand, accept, and explore our failures in order to leapfrog beyond them onto newer heights of success.

Of course, one of the first injuries found with failure is a swift moral injury to our ego. We often feel emboldened by this ego that we have ultimate control, and our failure has now become a part of our identity. The reality is that we can fail without any fault of our own. There can be many external factors that can influence us and our endeavors, and leave us at their mercy. For the factors that we may have been able to control, again our ego plays a hindering factor in allowing us to look beyond it in order to find the true cause of our failure.

I have often sat down and tried to understand the most intriguing aspects of failure, and that is to understand whether my failures have set me so far back that I may not recover, or whether they were just the crux of new beginnings, new beginnings which I would use to catapult myself and proceed to surpass all prior achievements. It is this dichotomy that leaves us sometimes in turmoil, when we stare at the mess we have just recently concocted.

I have come to the conclusion that perhaps the best way to approach setbacks in life is to understand that they are simply new beginnings. Whatever we were aspiring to accomplish or hell bent on achieving, perhaps these are simply redirections into a new beginning that will find us greater success. In essence, setbacks and failures are not the events themselves, but rather consider them to be the GPS navigator of our life, redirecting us on to our true chosen path without our knowledge.

That is where some people speak of a divine energy or a guiding force that is difficult to describe, often mysterious and unseen, that seems to always find us a way out of whatever predicaments we may be in. What is insightful is that often, these redirections found through setbacks seem so ambiguous, random, and unforeseen, at the moment in which they occur we are usually annoyed and irritated that something should dare move us from the path we were headed. Sometimes we can get so caught up in manifest destiny, in the human mind's desire to shape and control its surroundings, we rarely appreciate the miracles of failures and setbacks that guide us to a new truth.

How many times in your own lives have you set out determined to accomplish one specific objective, been sidetracked by resistance, and then found yourself working on something completely different yet infinitely more rewarding? That is the magic of life; it is always playing tricks on us, whether we choose to appreciate it or ignore it as a hindrance. This is where we find the common idea that is so prevalent, it is not the final destination that is important but rather the journey, as each journey is set with new beginnings, and each of those new beginnings shapes and guides us into where fate destined us to be.

So many discoveries, relationships, ideas, companies, and more are originated not by specific manifested goals, but rather stumbled upon clumsily by setbacks and failures that changed worldviews and allowed them to start new beginnings. It is these seemingly clumsy approaches that we have a setback or fail to accomplish our goals, become desperate and disparate, and then voila, we have a random idea that is seemingly foolish, but nonetheless we pursue it and start a new beginning. These seemingly clumsy approaches are very rarely as such; often, it is almost a majestic orchestra of a series of events that helps translate seemingly desperate failures into wonderful new beginnings.

Keep in mind that very rarely do these new beginnings translate into immediate success. Often these beginnings are humble, modest, and initiated with trepidation, as failure is immediately on the mind due to recency. It is these simple, humble, and new beginnings, as a result of a directional shift from setbacks, that launch us into stratospheric heights. As rarely anything in life has a set formula, it is very possible that these new beginnings can lead to setbacks and more subsequent shifts in direction. This is not unusual; in fact, it is quite normal to do so. Such is the nature of life that we often need to shift courses multiple times in order to find the right path in this journey we call life.

It is worthwhile to note that sometimes, life has certain intangibles which force us for various reasons, from economic, political, health, and so on, to initiate new beginnings. These are often done without any say from us, but rather we are thrust into the middle of a new, unsteady, and turbulent world which we have to make sense of. Through my poor health, I have been thrust into this scenario and am slowly, day by day adapting to the new reality that is set for me. I am sure at some future point, when all is settled, I will be thankful, as most usually are from new beginnings and opportunities which are difficult initially, but later in life, we see the value of the struggle and the fruits of our hard work.

One of the most important things that I have learned during these turbulent and difficult times is to accept the loss of control, and continue to ride the wave day by day. The ability to focus and get through each day is imperative when your world collapses around you. I write this as I am in a hospitable bed with one lung almost collapsed from fluid, and to be perfectly honest, I have found my peace. I understand that every day is a new journey, and I focus on getting through the days enjoying little victories and having complete faith that the future will unfold as it should, and my worries and anxieties are normal but fruitless, and will not help me define a new path in life. What is imperative is inner peace, strength, and truly believing that there will be a better life in this world or the next.

LEAVING DENTISTRY:
THIS WAY OUT

As appeared in DentalTown March 2021 edition.

For every dentist who's deeply and passionately in love with their profession, there's a plethora of dentists who can't wait for the day they get to retire their handpieces and run out of the dental office, never to be seen or heard from again. That's something few will admit, because who'd like to admit that they squandered almost eight years in school—and hundreds of thousands of dollars in tuition and student loan debt—only to be guaranteed to be perpetually miserable?

I call this the "professional pursuit of unhappiness." This is the forgotten and lost segment of our colleagues, because not only is it hard to share your displeasure, but the minute you do so you're often downplayed by perennially happy colleagues who can't wait to wake up to the smell of burned enamel in the morning. Then you're left wondering whether you're the single loser who can't appreciate the gifts of this fine profession, or your colleague who came back from a course after blowing thousands of dollars to finance the latest dental CE guru's yacht is from a different planet.

This is a demanding profession, and quite frankly, not all of us are cut out for the job. Unfortunately, many years of schooling, and often poor hands-on experience in school, lead few to have a good understanding on what they blew hundreds of thousands of dollars of the bank's money on. Add student loan debt a few years later, coupled with practice loan debt, and these poor anxiety-riddled souls are wondering in their office, as they waste the next three hours because of a no-show, whom they can thank for the woe they're living in day in and day out.

Acting the part, but feeling false

I bring this up because I started as an extremely passionate advocate of this profession—often going on multiple dental mission trips to work for free in sweaty jungles and orphanages, all in the name of doing some form of good. Over the years, it started to occur to me that perhaps my personality type was not suited for this, and I noticed a slow and steady erosion of my social skills and patience as I transformed from a happy-go-lucky person to a darker, more jaded soul.

Now, my patients always benefited from the best part of me, because I put on a brave face and gave them the best of me, even as they lied to me about their oral hygiene habits, while I smiled and nodded, completely "ignoring" the can of Mountain Dew they brought to their appointment.

The cost of that was a slow erosion of my soul. I met some wonderful people, had wonderful staff, and some great patients, yet deep inside was a sense of disenfranchisement that couldn't be quelled. I gave my heart and soul to the profession ,and yet I found it hollow and unfulfilling, despite that superficially I had achieved most levels of success in terms of a steady, happy patient pool, a wonderful, loyal staff, and a beautiful new clinic. Deep inside, though, I felt empty: a former shell of that once bright, excited young man who was overjoyed at opening his acceptance letter to dental school.

After my cancer treatment in August 2019, I recovered like a champion through sheer will and determination. I fought to regain my abilities to speak, eat, and chew and came rushing back to work within six weeks. What I learned the difficult way after returning back to work was that even though I had changed, nothing around me had; my circumstances remained the same. This meant the mental anguish that once was palpable was now insufferable, because my mind had not adjusted to the trauma it had endured. What was even worse was that in my mind, this trauma was unjust, because I had no risk factor and like any well-trained dental professional, I avoided all of the known risk factors of oral cancer. That felt almost ironic at this point: the shoemaker whose own shoe was broken.

As I struggled through these mental demons, I witnessed the world descend into the beginnings of what would later evolve into a worldwide pandemic. Somewhere in the chaos of shutting down my clinic and figuring out what to do with my staff, patients, and the clinic, I noticed a swelling in my jaw on the same side I had my surgery and neck dissection. Just a week prior, my best friend and dentist had performed some dental fillings, and after the procedure my neck had swollen up. Not to take anything lightly, I called my ENT surgeon immediately to schedule a biopsy and CT scans to confirm.

Another health challenge

On April Fool's Day, I got a call from my ENT that the biopsy came back positive for cancer. It appeared that they had missed a lymph node from my first surgery. I would require a second surgery, subsequent chemotherapy, and radiation in the middle of a pandemic and lockdown. I was then placed in quarantine to be safe before the surgery, and two days later, I found out that my grandmother had passed away.

Still in shock with all the bad news, I managed to make it through the next surgery, and realized during my recovery that the mental and emotional toll was far too great for me to be able to manage my clinic to the best of my abilities while healing. So, I made the difficult decision to sell the clinic in which I had invested so much of myself at great personal cost to build from scratch and make a success.

I decided to sell the clinic myself, and while recovering from surgery, I completed a dozen showings before finding the right individual with whom I was fortunate to share the same morals and values. I was blessed to find a buyer in the pandemic who did not in any way take advantage of my situation, and was a pleasure to work with during the sale process.

As my clinic sale continued, I started my radiation and chemotherapy, which involved 33 treatments over the course of seven long weeks, whereby I had to visit the hospital every Monday to Friday. The pandemic precautions made this difficult process even more arduous; I was not allowed visitors during my treatments and consultations, and had to face these all alone, which was not easy, but like most challenges in life, was not insurmountable with the right attitude.

The chemo and radiation treatments were extremely difficult to bear with—probably some of the most difficult and arduous days of my life. However, as they say, this too shall pass, and in due time it did, and truly what didn't kill me only made me infinitely stronger.

Time to say goodbye to dentistry

After years of pondering whether dentistry was for me, I was basically granted my wish of an early release—"honorable discharge," if you will. Here I was, free of all my responsibilities and worries, recovering from some traumatic events—and at this point, you'd think that I would've been deeply upset about the sense of loss and purpose. In this regard you would be incorrect.

I felt such a deep sense of relief and release of tension—as if a great weight had been lifted off my shoulders. Over time, people around me noticed a great change in my personality. I felt more relaxed, calmer, just a better person overall. The fault was never with my profession; the fault was that I recognized the inner conflict, yet never had the courage to do something about it. Unfortunately, it took a life-changing event to forcibly thrust me into a different frame of mind, and for that—despite the pain and turmoil—I am deeply grateful.

As I transition into a new life devoid of handpieces and hygiene checks, I find myself excited to explore all that is around me, and to engage the sense of self that died a long time ago as I was forced to put on a mask and pretend to be someone that I wasn't. The tremendous debt and commitment required for us to reach our accreditation sometimes buries us with the fear and shame of moving on when we realize this path is not for us. My only thought remaining was not, "Why did this happen to me?" but rather, "Why did I not act on this sooner?" The dark but beautiful side of facing your mortality at an early age is that you realize death is the only ever-present factor, and it respects no boundaries. The sooner we come to terms with this fact, the faster we can embrace our inner selves and take full advantage of the precious years we may have left.

In summary, if you deeply feel that what you are doing goes against every fiber in your body, spend some time doing some soul-searching as to why you're actually there. You will be surprised that most of us have chosen our paths without an in-depth analysis as to what we actually want, and hence we are left with a deep sense of unfulfillment. This can lead you into two paths: on one, you realize your original sense of purpose and your why, which can lead you to a renewed sense of fulfilment. The other can identify a glaring gap between your present choices and your true need for fulfillment, and you realize that on your current journey, the two will never meet.

EPILOGUE:
DR. PARUL DUA MAKKAR

Dear Reader,

Now that you have read these series of blogs, let me introduce you to the writer, Dr. Manu Dua, my little brother.

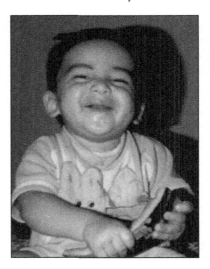

Manu was born in Abu Dhabi, U.A.E to Indian parents. They had moved from India in hopes for a better future for their children. Manu was born when I was 7 and a half. I have watched him grow up from a cute baby to a toddler with dimples, from days of rummaging through my toys, coloring over my home-work, splashes in the bathtub, and splashing in swim meets. He was entrusted to my care since the day he was born. I tied my first Rakhi to a 2-month-old baby. That moment, in a two-bedroom apartment on the 6th floor of the Dunhill Building, is forever etched in my brain: the day I tied and solidified the bond between a brother and a sister with a thread.

Manu had a happy childhood. He grew up in the Desert heat playing rugby, swimming, building Legos and sandcastles on the beach.

Each summer, we flew to India and spent time with our grand-parents and extended family of uncles, aunts, and cousins. Flying kites on roof tops, eating street food and getting sick, spending days shopping for bargains on streets of Delhi at Connaught Place. Exploring the cities of Delhi and Agra, and the vast Indian culture and history. We were also lucky enough to have the opportunity to travel the world across Europe and Asia. Manu was just a little boy when we took him to Europe. I have memories of pushing his stroller all over the cobblestones of European cities, getting lost in Turkey, and eating on banana leaves in Singapore. One of our last trips together, the four of us went on a road trip around the United States, using the folded-out maps in the days before GPS and smartphones. It was on this trip he met his favorite, Mickey Mouse at Disney World, and when he gave him the biggest hug, Manu's face lit up. This was the trip right before I started college.

I left for college in the United States, and this tween developed into a handsome young man.

In my days of higher education, from Undergrad to Dental school, he migrated to Canada with my parents. He had the front seat to the migration, and my parents' struggle and their challenges. He never let me forget their trials and tribulations. He was only thirteen, and I was not there to help him adjust to a new country, culture, and way of life. He grew up with harsh realities of being short in stature, brown, and a new immigrant kid in middle school, with parents who themselves were trying to navigate their way into a new world. Did I mention going from 40 C to -40 C? Yet despite all the hardships, he excelled in all sports and graduated high school with honors. He developed a knack for working with his hands in welding class while building intricate structures which were often displayed. He still spoke highly of his Biology and English teachers who guided him and helped mold his final days of high school. He found his way back to the rugby field as a player and a coach to young kids, and his team won the Provincial championship. He also started to ice skate, play ice hockey, and snowboard.

Manu was my mother's companion in the days of Calgary Stampede, accompanying her on the early morning breakfasts. He was also her partner on the Badminton court. Mom and Manu would spend hours in the kitchen, trying new cuisines and recipes. He was my dad's golf partner, and the one to help him understand all the modern gizmos and gadgets in the world of ever changing technology. Manu would be the one to watch all the latest movies with our dad, explaining and re-explaining plot twists. Manu was also an avid reader, and he never lost his zest for reading. He devoured self-help books, financial books, and was a history buff and fan of Tom Clancy and Tin Tin. He had a passion for such a vast array of genres of books, and soaked in the information. From these he drew aspirations of what he wanted to accomplish in life.

During his few years of Undergrad at the University of Calgary, he found his Indian roots. He forged new friendships and a love for Punjabi music and dancing Bhangra. Manu had no match on the dance floor. If there was good music, Manu's feet would be found dancing away. Always a foodie, he loved exploring new recipes in the kitchen and trying out new restaurants wherever he travelled. Whenever he visited us, he would research restaurants to go to. It wasn't about the fanciest, but the one with the yummiest food. In college, he was a business major, but decided to follow my footsteps into Dentistry at University of British Columbia in Vancouver.

Life wasn't easy for Manu in Dental School. His first year he spent in crutches due to an ACL repair surgery over the summer. He was discouraged by some of his professors, who even asked him to drop out. He was told that he couldn't be a successful dentist, and to opt for a different career choice. Regardless, he was determined. Not only did he get through with friends and with the help of some good assistants that pushed him more to excel, he also helped people along the way. He stayed determined on this goal, and graduated with a DMD at the age of 26. Boy, did he prove everyone wrong!

When he graduated in 2012, my parent's pride was palpable. They had my maternal grandparents flown from India for the graduation. They were the quintessential immigrant success story, well-settled in Calgary with two kids who were doctors. My parents were already grandparents to my son, with another along the way, and my parents were looking forward to another celebration: Manu's wedding. "The natural order of things."

After graduation, Manu worked diligently. He worked in remote areas of Alberta to gain knowledge and experience. He had the spirit of my parents ingrained in him: to work hard, honestly, and ethically with integrity. His achievements have been his own, in life, in sports, in academics, in dentistry, and in his art of writing. He may have followed my path, but made his own unique footprints. He took big strides. He was bold, precise, calculative, and determined. He excelled in whatever he put his mind to and built his own success story. He fostered his love of fast cars and good food. He had a 2nd ACL tear, but his injuries did not stop him from being on the golf course or badminton court. Manu paid off all his student loans and opened up a start-up practice in Calgary in the middle of recession in 2016. It was not an easy feat, and he did it all on his own. From laying out plans with contractors, fighting for permits, painting, furnishing, building a website, tando marketing, this was his baby, and he was so proud. He built a great reputation for himself. He was well liked, admired, and respected among his patients and staff. At work, he was known to do the Hail Mary play, making every last effort to overcome tough cases and situations. In his spare time, he found it in him to help the community. He would volunteer time at Calgary Urban Projects Society (CUPS) providing free dental care to the homeless. He also travelled to Peru on mission trips, taking time out of his own practice to help the underprivileged. This to him was so rewarding, to help those who didn't have access to proper health care. Posthumously, his clinic was awarded Platinum winner in the Best Dentists section by the community in Calgary, Alberta.

Manu was a happy-go-lucky man; he was kind, compassionate, patient, and a joy to have around. He had a charismatic personality with an infectious laugh, fond of good company, food, and close friends with a great sense of humor.

He always had the best interest at heart for everyone, and was never shy to speak his mind. He lived life on his own terms, never to mold to others' expectations and ideals. That was a very commendable quality of his. He was brave, optimistic, never afraid of a challenge, resilient, and pushed through every obstacle. He was admired and respected not only in Calgary, but also among his peers around the US, Canada, and on DentalTown (online Dental community), so much so that he did podcasts and was featured with his practice on the cover of the DentalTown magazine in November 2019. This article was featured after his first cancer surgery, and it chronicled his business model, his startup, and his cancer journey. After this, he was asked to be a speaker at a few Dental Meetings in the US and Canada. He had another article published in the DentalTown magazine in March 2021 that got printed posthumously. The title: Leaving Dentistry: This Way Out.

Manu was an inspiration to many, including me. He helped guide me to building my own practice. In September 2019, a month after his first surgery, he came to New York to visit and help me navigate hurdles to new ownership. You see, even though he was the younger brother, Manu was wise beyond his years. He had been molded by his life, struggles, and cancer. He gained a new perspective in life when faced with his own mortality. He was my lighthouse, guiding me the right way. My relentless champion.

Manu was a fighter, true to his inner self. He fought a tough battle against cancer. He had plenty of scars to prove the rounds of surgery, immunotherapy, chemotherapy, and radiation. He also had scars that could not be seen. Those which my parents bear as well. I felt that Manu was a victim of the Canadian Health

System. There were so many opportunities for physicians to successfully respond to Manu's cancer, but they were lost in the Health System. In early June 2019, he showed me a lesion on his tongue, and I urged him to get a biopsy. It was a decent size at the time, but manageable. He said that his Oral Surgeon thought that it was Lichen Planus (a non-malignant lesion), and wasn't worried that it could be a malignant lesion, as Manu was healthy, young, and did not have any risk factors. Manu was given steroids for Lichen Planus before the biopsy, before confirming what the lesion was. He even had his wisdom teeth pulled later in June, but never had the biopsy. I went to visit him in July, and by then the lesion had grown substantially. The biopsy was delayed until the end of July, and by then the lesion had become Stage 2 Oral cancer (squamous cell). He had a multi-8-hour surgery in August 2019. He had an amazing team of doctors, Plastic Surgeons, ENTs, Oral Surgeons, and more. However, he had no pathologist who checked if all the cancer cells from lymph nodes were removed at the time of the surgery. While in the hospital, he developed an abscess and swelling three days post surgery, yet the attending nurse would not help him. She passed it off as a post op swelling. He had to help himself survive and contact a plastic surgeon on call. His breathing tube from the tracheotomy was dislodged, and he almost lost his life there if they had not gotten it in time. He did not have any further scans, and was not given any radiation treatment post-surgery. Just after surgery, because he was mentally and physically strong, he bounced back. After visiting me in New York in September, by October 2019 he was back at work seeing patients.

He had a new lease on life. He bought a Porsche, got a dog, and he was starting to check off items on his bucket list.

He was so excited to have beaten cancer, and we had planned a trip to Hawaii to celebrate his recovery and our father's 70th birthday. A trip to a warm place, another bucket list item. Manu was planning to relocate to Arizona, Texas, or California after recovering to escape the harsh winters of Calgary. Later in April of 2020, just when COVID-19 a worldwide Pandemic, hit, he had a swelling in his lymph nodes post-dental treatment. The cancer had returned, and as we found out later, with a vengeance. It was suggested that there were some cancer cells that were missed from initial surgery, thus the recurrence within 8 months. Since he didn't have any radiation or chemotherapy, it was left untreated. In April, we also found out that he even had a small lesion on the lung on the same side as he had on his tongue. He also had a cough, and the lung lesion was written off as an effect due to a cough. Thus, no PET scans were done to check, nor was a biopsy of the lungs enforced to check for Metastasis. The Hawaii family trip was cancelled due to COVID and he was back in the operating room in April. Amidst all this, our maternal grandmother passed that same month. This was a devastating compounded loss to all of us.

After the cancer reappeared and Manu mentally prepared himself for the second surgery, he made a conscious decision to support his health, and he decided to sell his practice. He had plans to write this book, to travel, to present his journey. He aspired to run a mobile clinic for elderly, and to be a business property owner. All these dreams have been interrupted. His 34th birthday, June 2020, was spent undergoing chemo and radiation.

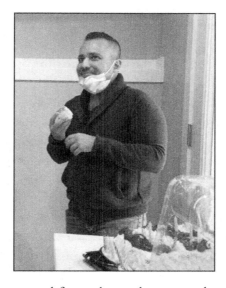

Once he recovered from chemotherapy and radiation, he sold his practice, and planned on living life to its fullest on his terms. In those months after July, those around him thought he was the happiest he had ever been. He spent weekends kayaking, golfing, or driving around his Porsche. He was back to playing sports. He kept busy building large Lego pieces and reading. He was high on life. I was unable to visit because at that time, New York was a hot spot for COVID, and he was immunocompromised. None of us wanted to risk my travel with his recovery. Manu was to have a follow-up for the lung lesion in October 2020 with CT scans, but It was delayed to November. That is when he found out that the lesion in the lungs had grown four times the size. The cancer was on his lung lining, and was deemed inoperable. A PET scan was finally done, and showed the cancer spread as far out as his left pelvic bone. From then on, his prognosis worsened and took a downward spiral. In December, he was admitted for shortness of breath, and they found fluid in his lungs. The fluid was positive for cancer cells, all before his scheduled lung biopsy date. Thereafter, he went a few times in one week to have fluid drained until he finally had a port placed in his chest for fluid draining. The port wasn't placed properly, and he complained for months in agonizing pain. As he had been through so much, he had requested an experienced surgeon, yet a resident did the surgery. The surgeon had been rough, manipulating him to place his chest port, thus he suffered a lot of pain and discomfort upon eating, breathing, sitting, and lying down. My MD friends in New York pushed me to go see him, as he was on borrowed time. I visited him in December, not knowing it was the last time I would see him alive. We made life-after-cancer plans to travel. My parents wanted to give him a business class trip to his destination of choice.

My parents supported him and nursed him, getting Manu to doctor visits, blood work, hospital admissions, taking him for scans, getting his medications, taking him to chemotherapy, radiation therapy, immunotherapy, buying and making any special food, anything that would help Manu. They watched their young, vibrant son wither before their eyes without being able to help him. Manu was admitted for high Calcium levels New Year's eve of 2021. I prayed he wouldn't spend New Year at the hospital. Manu had full palliative care at home: a hospital bed, wheelchair, and pain management treatment. Among COVID restrictions, taking time off work, and with not much family or help due to restrictions, my parents were in the vacuum of Manu. The doctors tried the latest therapies and experimental drugs, essentially shooting in the dark, hoping that something would work. Modern medicine and the Canadian Health System had failed Manu, and he knew he was dying. He was unable to eat, losing his appetite, and he was unable to sit comfortably. He was hardly sleeping due to unbearable pain from the port placement. He had no desire to go out, as the cold Alberta air hurt his lungs. He had difficulty breathing and barely spoke.

In January of 2021, he was back in the hospital for abdominal swelling. He spent 2 weeks alone in hospital with no visitors, getting IV antibiotics for the swelling. He was released, but still complained of pain at the port site. He would drain close to 1 L of fluid from his lungs every day from December till the day he passed. After months of complaining, his port was removed and placed in a new spot in February. A new swelling appeared at the site of the first port, so the doctors kept subjecting him to an array of antibiotics, treating it without knowing what it was. Due to COVID, he wasn't allowed to have anyone with him for his consults with the doctors. Imagine his strength going through it alone. He was losing weight rapidly, and the antibiotics were taking a toll. He had diarrhea and vomiting. He had no energy left to fight, but he still had the will. We talked about having his blogs published. He told me to wait while he was in the hospital. "Don't rush, we have time! I want to write more."

Weeks after being admitted and no antibiotic working, he called me on February 25th from the hospital while I was at work. He told me there were high potassium levels and the mass on the side of his abdomen was finally biopsied. It was not an infection, it was positive for cancer. I broke down, and he stayed strong for me. He had made peace and had accepted his fate. He was to get radiation therapy to help with the pain. I made plans to visit on March 20th, once he would be done with radiation treatment. A week before my scheduled trip, on Friday the 12th, my dad said Manu had leg swelling due to clots with shortness of breath, and was being admitted. On the evening 13th of March, my parents called me to tell me that they met with the whole team, and Manu has now moved to hospice. I was told he may not have a week to when I was coming. "Come home now!" On March 14th 2021, while I scampered to get COVID tested results expedited by my physician and booked a flight for the next day, I was informed that he was going into organ failure. I was asked to say my goodbye via video call on WhatsApp. He was sedated, barely conscious. My husband and I told him not to hold on for us, he does not need to suffer anymore. We will be ok. It's okay to let go. Go if you need to go, we love you. Later in the day, I got my results and booked my flight. I was going home. A few hours later, while I packed for the trip home, I got the dreaded call. He had taken his last breaths with our parents by his side. I was a day too late.

On that day, the most unnatural thing happened. A dad out-lived his son, a mother could not wake up her son, a sister could not say goodbye in person. That day, I lost my brother and was left with the shells of my parents. That day, our God died, and all joy was sucked from our world. As a parent myself, I cannot fathom that pain, hurt, and that gaping wound. A parent's worst nightmare to outlive and cremate their child. I watched on a video call as my parents hugged and kissed their deceased son. I watched through my tears, my husband holding me, the last goodbye. I had nothing, not even words, to comfort my parents nor the ability to even hold them. My dad did not realize the moment that he passed, even though he was right there with him. My mom was staying strong for us all, even though she had lost her mother and son in less than a year. After I got off the video call with my parents, I was imagining that trip back home after leaving my brother to be taken to the morgue. That trip to come home to a dark and empty house without him, knowing that he will never come home. My elderly parents were forced to make that trip alone. They had lost the battle against cancer, against destiny, against hope, against time.

My brother had confided in his close friends that he was done for, that death was better than this life of pain. I think he could have survived or had more time if there was an earlier diagnosis, or if there was a PET scan when the lung lesion was first discovered. If he had chemo and radiation after his first surgery, if the doctors treated the cancer aggressively. If there was more that was done to help him survive. A man who was so giving, talented, gifted, brilliant in every way left this Earth. A man who loved life and had so much to offer the world. A man who could light up the room with his smile and kind eyes. Hindsight is always 2020. We are left with what-ifs. We try to make sense of senseless tragedies, of the bigger plan. Maybe we are narrow minded, living in our bubbles, selfish for our own needs so we cannot see the meaning of it all. This was the time for my parents to enjoy the fruit of the labors and sacrifices, to enjoy their grandkids, but now they were picking out a casket and making funeral arrangements for their youngest child. Sitting there planning it all with my parents was the most isolating feeling in the world. I felt so alone. My family had just died with him. A part of my identity as an older sister died. How can I ever say those words, I had a brother. My kids will grow up not knowing their uncle or have more cousins. Nothing can prepare you for this moment, no matter how much you know of the prognosis. There's an immense void, void of joy, void of laughter, void of Manu. A void that can never be filled. The day after the cremation, it was hard to accept the sun rising again and life going on. Everything was the same, except Manu was no longer a part of this world.

In the time of his greatest pain, Manu penned his thoughts. He could not talk, as it hurt, so he expressed himself in words. I am glad that he did. It gives insight to what he was going through. He had come to terms with his fate, and he was at peace. I would like to share these thoughts with you. These thoughts are of a young man who had so much to give, who was more than the disease that took him. He left the world in a better place. He was the greatest gift my parents gave me. In the 2 years of his battle, he showed me so much strength, restraint, dignity, and class. He was the pride of my amazing parents. Our parents gave up so much for our future. They left their home for a better life for us. They are the best parents that a child could hope for, always forgiving, always there, always pushing us to be our absolute best. Selfless, putting our needs over their own. I could never even come close to giving them back what they gave me.

Manu was the witness to the life we once had. From India to Abu Dhabi, to Doha back to Abu Dhabi, to the United States and finally to Calgary. From sandy beaches to snow covered mountains. He was to give me nieces and nephews, to outlive me, but life has been unjust and unkind. He touched a lot of people. After he passed, I was overwhelmed with the people that reached out to us via emails, calls, texts. People who were our friends, family, his friends, alma mater, fellow dentists, online Dental groups, patients, staff, and even strangers who learnt of his passing. His impact on this world was immense even though he had a short life.

Many people whose loved ones or they themselves have fought cancer have reached out to me, but they did not have a voice like Manu's. I would like to thank the countless people, our friends, family, doctors to whom I reached out for help, advice, and guidance, those who were there no matter the time, or who may have been battling their own battles. I am eternally grateful to Manu's friends who defined true friendship by staying with him till his last days. Those who called, messaged, and came to visit him whenever they could, even during COVID. I am thankful for my husband, who was my rock in keeping my sanity and who put my pieces back together every time I fell apart. My kids, who give me a renewed purpose. My in-laws, who gave me space to grieve.

Hope you find comfort and wisdom in his words if you or your loved one must walk this path.

To my dearest Manu,

Then, I carried you in my arms, now I carry you in my heart.

You are done fighting. Now rest baby brother. Your fight may be over but not your journey. You will continue to live through your words.

And in my next life may I be so privileged to call you my brother.

Till we meet again,
Love, Didi*

*Older Sister

Printed in Great Britain
by Amazon

10903118R00054